D1540482

LIFE
ON MISSION
A Simple Way to
SHARE THE GOSPEL

DUSTIN WILLIS | AARON COE
Foreword by DAVID PLATT

LifeWay Press®
Nashville, Tennessee

Published by LifeWay Press® • © 2014 Dustin Willis and Aaron Coe

No part of this book may be reproduced or transmitted in any form or by any means, electronic or mechanical, including photocopying and recording, or by any information storage or retrieval system, except as may be expressly permitted in writing by the publisher. Requests for permission should be addressed in writing to LifeWay Press®; One LifeWay Plaza; Nashville, TN 37234-0152.

ISBN 978-1-4300-3946-4 • Item 005717345

Dewey decimal classification: 269.2
Subject heading: EVANGELISTIC WORK \ WITNESSING \ MISSIONS

Unless otherwise indicated, all Scripture quotations are taken from the Holman Christian Standard Bible®, Copyright © 1999, 2000, 2002, 2003, 2009 by Holman Bible Publishers. Used by permission. Holman Christian Standard Bible®, Holman CSB®, and HCSB® are federally registered trademarks of Holman Bible Publishers. Scripture quotations marked ESV are taken from The Holy Bible, English Standard Version® (ESV®), copyright © 2001 by Crossway, a publishing ministry of Good News Publishers. Used by permission. All rights reserved. Scripture quotations marked NIV are taken from the Holy Bible, NEW INTERNATIONAL VERSION®. Copyright © 1973, 1978, 1984 by Biblica Inc. All rights reserved worldwide. Used by permission. Scripture quotations marked NASB are taken from the New American Standard Bible®, Copyright © 1960, 1962, 1963, 1968, 1971, 1972, 1973, 1975, 1977, 1995 by The Lockman Foundation. Used by permission. (www.lockman.org)

To order additional copies of this resource, write to LifeWay Church Resources Customer Service; One LifeWay Plaza; Nashville, TN 37234-0113; fax 615.251.5933; phone toll free 800.458.2772; email orderentry@lifeway.com; order online at www.lifeway.com; or visit the LifeWay Christian Store serving you.

Printed in the United States of America

Adult Ministry Publishing • LifeWay Church Resources • One LifeWay Plaza • Nashville, TN 37234-0152

CONTENTS

Dedicated to the thousands of missionaries
who work hard every day to make Jesus known in
North America, many of whom are doing so without
great fanfare and without much financial reward.

One hundred percent of the royalties from
this Bible study will directly support missionaries
in North America through Send North America.

THE AUTHORS

AARON COE @AARONBCOE

Aaron Coe serves as the vice president of mobilization and marketing at the North American Mission Board, providing leadership in mobilizing churches and missionaries to plant churches. He and his wife, Carmen, have four children, Ezra James, Danielle, Joshua, and Harper. Aaron blogs at **aaronbcoe.com** and is a regular contributor at **sendnetwork.com.**

DUSTIN WILLIS @DUSTINWILLIS

Dustin Willis serves as the coordinator of the Send Network and the Send North America Conference. Dustin lives in metro Atlanta with his wife, Renie, and their two children, Jack and Piper. Before moving to Atlanta, Dustin planted and pastored Midtown Fellowship in Columbia, South Carolina. Dustin blogs at **dustinwillis.com** and is a regular contributor at **sendnetwork.com.**

SEND》NETWORK

Your life has a mission. We want to see you succeed in this mission, whether by leading a church, planting a church, or living on mission in your everyday life. The Send Network was established to deliver resources and provide opportunities that equip you and your church with the gospel and that mobilize you to be on mission in your local community and beyond.

SENDNETWORK.COM

ACKNOWLEDGMENTS

A Bible study like this is the product of the ideas of countless people. Though two people had the opportunity to write the study, hundreds of people contributed to its fruition.

Threaded throughout the pages of this study you will find an incredible tool called Three Circles. Three Circles is a simple way to take life conversations and turn them into gospel conversations.

Our good friend Pastor Jimmy Scroggins and the people of Family Church in West Palm Beach, Florida, have not only generously given this tool away through this study and through the Life Conversation Guide but have also boldly shared the gospel by using Three Circles all over south Florida and throughout the world. Jimmy, thank you for your boldness, zeal, and sacrifice in advancing the gospel.

Learn more about Family Church in West Palm Beach, Florida, at **gofamilychurch.org.**

FOREWORD

DAVID PLATT

Ordinary people with extraordinary power preaching, praying, giving, and suffering for the spread of the gospel.

This is the picture of the early church we see on the pages of the New Testament. A small band of 12 men responded to Jesus' life-changing invitation: "Follow me, and I will make you fishers of men" (Matt. 4:19, ESV). In the days to come, they watched Jesus, listened to Him, and learned from Him how to love, teach, and serve others the same way He did. Then came the moment when they saw Him die on a cross for their sins, only to rise from the dead three days later. Soon He gathered them on a mountainside and issued this call:

> All authority has been given to Me in heaven and on earth.
> Go, therefore, and make disciples of all nations, baptizing them
> in the name of the Father and of the Son and of the Holy Spirit,
> teaching them to observe everything I have commanded you.
> And remember, I am with you always, to the end of the age.
> **MATTHEW 28:18-20**

Just as Jesus had said from the beginning, these followers would now become fishers of men. His authoritative commission would become their consuming ambition.

Later Jesus' disciples gathered with a small group of other Christ followers, about 120 in all, and they waited. True to His promise, Jesus sent His Spirit to every one of them, and immediately they began proclaiming the gospel. In the days to come, they scattered from Jerusalem to Judea to Samaria to the ends of the earth (see Acts 1:8), and within one generation they grew to over four hundred times the size they were when they started. How did this happen?

The spread of the gospel in the Book of Acts took place primarily because ordinary people, empowered by an extraordinary presence, proclaimed the gospel everywhere they went. To be sure, God appointed well-known apostles like Peter, John, and Paul for certain positions of leadership in the church. Yet it was anonymous Christians who first took the gospel to Judea and Samaria, and it was unnamed believers who founded the church in Antioch, which became a base for the mission to the Gentile world. It was unidentified followers of Jesus who spread the gospel throughout all of Asia. Disciples were made and churches were multiplied in places the apostles never went. The good news of Jesus spread not just through gifted preachers but through everyday people whose lives had been transformed by the power of Christ. They went from house to house and to marketplaces and shops along streets and travel routes, leading people to faith in Jesus on a daily basis.

This is how the gospel penetrated the world during the first century: through self-denying, Spirit-empowered disciples of Jesus who were making disciples of Jesus. Followers of Jesus were fishing for men. Disciples were making disciples. Christians weren't known for casual association with Christ and His church; instead, they were known for complete abandonment to Christ and His cause. The Great Commission wasn't a choice for them to consider but a command for them to obey. And though they faced untold trials and unthinkable persecution, they experienced unimaginable joy as they joined Jesus to advance His kingdom.

I want to be part of a movement like that. I want to be part of a people who really believe we have the Spirit of God in each of us for the spread of the gospel through all of us. I want to be part of a people who gladly sacrifice the pleasures, pursuits, and possessions of this world because we're living for treasure in the world to come. I want to be part of a people who forsake every earthly ambition in favor of one eternal aspiration: to see disciples made and churches multiplied from our houses to our communities to our cities to the nations.

This kind of movement involves all of us. Every follower of Christ fishing for men. Every disciple making disciples. Ordinary people spreading the gospel in extraordinary ways all over the world. Men and women from diverse backgrounds with different gifts and distinct platforms making disciples and multiplying churches through every domain of society in every place on the planet. This is God's design for His church, and disciples of Jesus mustn't settle for anything less.

That's what this Bible study is all about. Dustin Willis and Aaron Coe explain biblical foundations and explore practical implications of the way God has designed your life to be part of His purpose in the world. As you study and apply these truths, I encourage you to join God's work in your neighborhood, in North America, and among the nations for the sake of His great name.

HOW TO USE THIS STUDY

Life on Mission provides five weeks of study. Each week is divided into sections for group interaction and personal study. After your first group session, you'll complete a week of daily, personal study before the next group session.

START

The first section of each group session includes initial icebreakers and group discussion designed to spark conversation and introduce the topic of the session.

WATCH

The Watch section of each session provides key statements for participants to follow during the video interview.

RESPOND

The final component of the group session provides discussion questions related to the video interview teaching and offers an opportunity for learners to share and grow together.

PERSONAL STUDY

The individual component of the study offers five short, interactive devotions for use each week between group sessions. Complete the devotions and learning activities before attending the group session related to that topic.

Your life on mission matters. How you spend these moments with God will determine just how much. Use the two parts of this material—group and personal study—as necessary preparation for your life on mission.

TIPS FOR LEADING A GROUP

PRAYERFULLY PREPARE

Prepare for each session by—

> reviewing the weekly material and group questions ahead of time;

> praying for each person in the group.

Ask the Holy Spirit to work through you and the group discussion as you point to Jesus each week through God's Word.

MINIMIZE DISTRACTIONS

Create a comfortable environment. If group members are uncomfortable, they'll be distracted and therefore unengaged in the group experience. Plan ahead by taking into consideration—

> seating;

> temperature and lighting;

> food or drink;

> surrounding noise;

> general cleanliness (put pets away if meeting in a home).

At best, thoughtfulness and hospitality show guests and group members they're welcome and valued in whatever environment you choose to gather. At worst, people may never notice your effort, but they're also not distracted. Do everything in your ability to help people focus on what's most important: connecting with God, with the Bible, and with others.

INCLUDE OTHERS

Your goal is to foster a community in which people are welcome just as they are but encouraged to grow spiritually. Always be aware of opportunities to—

> **INVITE** new people to join your group;

> **INCLUDE** any people who visit the group.

An inexpensive way to make first-time guests feel welcome or to invite people to get involved is to give them their own copies of this Bible study book.

ENCOURAGE DISCUSSION

A good small group gathering has the following characteristics.

> **EVERYONE PARTICIPATES.** Encourage everyone to ask questions, share responses, or read aloud.

> **NO ONE DOMINATES—NOT EVEN THE LEADER.** Be sure what you say takes up less than half of your time together as a group. Politely redirect discussion if anyone dominates.

> **NOBODY IS RUSHED THROUGH QUESTIONS.** Don't feel that a moment of silence is a bad thing. People often need time to think about their responses to questions they've just heard or to gain courage to share what God is stirring in their hearts.

> **INPUT IS AFFIRMED AND FOLLOWED UP.** Make sure you point out something true or helpful in a response. Don't just move on. Build personal connections with follow-up questions, asking how other people have experienced similar things or how a truth has shaped their understanding of God and the Scripture you're studying. People are less likely to speak up if they fear that you don't actually want to hear their answers or that you're looking for only a certain answer.

> **GOD AND HIS WORD ARE CENTRAL.** Opinions and experiences can be helpful, but God has given us the truth. Trust Scripture to be the authority and God's Spirit to work in people's lives. You can't change anyone, but God can. Continually point people to the Word and to active steps of faith.

KEEP CONNECTING

Think of ways to connect with group members during the week. Participation during the group session is always improved when members spend time connecting with one another away from the session. The more people are comfortable with and involved in one another's lives, the more they'll look forward to being together. When people move beyond being friendly and in the same group to truly being friends who form a community, they come to each session eager to engage instead of merely attending.

Encourage group members with thoughts, commitments, or questions from the session by connecting through—

> emails;
> texts;
> social media.

When possible, build deeper friendships by planning or spontaneously inviting group members to join you outside your regularly scheduled group time for—

> meals;
> fun activities;
> projects around your home, church, or community.

SESSION 1

START

If this is your first time meeting together as a group or if anybody has recently joined the group, take a moment for people to introduce themselves.

Start the group session by asking everyone the following question.

> *If people described you with a single word, phrase, or activity, what would it be?*

After everyone has had a chance to respond, follow up by asking these questions.

> *Do you think most people would be able to describe you by accurately identifying a characteristic or an activity that you value?*

> *Would anyone also like to describe themselves with an interest, ability, or characteristic that may not be as familiar to people?*

Transition to the video with the following thought.

Today we'll begin looking at ways each of us can use our different interests, abilities, and areas of influence for a common purpose. God is inviting each of us to join His great redemptive work by living life on mission.

LIFE ON MISSION

WATCH

Follow the notes below as you watch this week's video featuring Ronnie Floyd.

- In dealing with today's culture, be courageous but wise.

- Be involved in the community.

- The real motivation is that Christ came to redeem the world.

- We have been given the Holy Spirit's power, and we're to be witnesses wherever we are, whatever we may do.

- Everyone has influence.

- God has created us to extend His glory to the nations, to make a difference and know that God can use us.

Scripture references: Matthew 28:19-20; Acts 1:8; John 20:21

Three Circles, shown below, is a simple conversation guide for your life on mission.

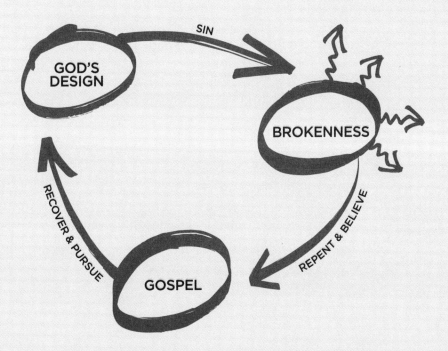

RESPOND

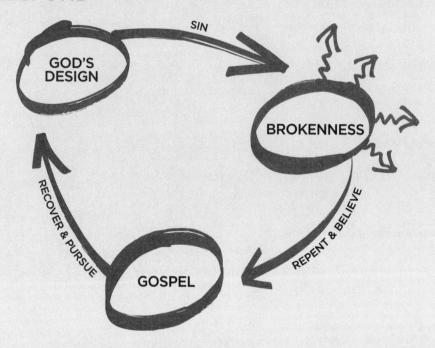

The next four sessions will focus on clearly understanding and comfortably discussing Three Circles. The goal is to have natural conversations about your faith in daily life.

How often do you talk about your faith? Share the gospel?

What prevents you from talking about God's design, our brokenness, and the gospel?

Ronnie said, "In dealing with today's culture, be courageous but wise."

What are some examples of being courageous but unwise? How can you be both courageous and wise in interacting with people?

LIFE ON MISSION

Before this session what did you honestly think of when you heard the word mission?

Has your understanding changed? If so, how?

How would you define the mission of God?

Ask three people to read aloud Matthew 28:19-20; Acts 1:8; John 20:21.

Which of Jesus' words most convict, challenge, or encourage you to live life on mission? Why?

How can you use your influence in your community to be involved in God's redemptive mission?

Whom did God use to share the gospel with you? Share a brief story of the way you came to faith in Christ.

When has God used you to share the gospel? Share a brief story.

Wrap up the session with any final questions or observations before closing with prayer. Thank God for redeeming you and inviting you to join His mission.

Use the next page to record ideas, questions, or prayers.

Complete the personal study in "God's Design" (pp. 19–35) before the next group session.

PERSONAL STUDY

GOD'S DESIGN

INTRODUCTION

"In the beginning God ..."
GENESIS 1:1

The first words of Scripture reveal the ultimate foundation for life on mission. God is the giver of life. He alone is worth of our worship. Nothing else in this world can satisfy the longing of our hearts. People need to know this life-changing truth.

But many people don't know it. People aren't worshiping God. And we're not just talking about strangers in remote villages around the planet. We're talking about people around you every day—neighbors, friends, coworkers, classmates, even family members. Many people who are part of your daily life don't have the abundant, eternal life found only in a relationship with God.

God's design for our lives, His desire for all creation, has been broken by humanity's selfish pursuit of sin. Only the hope of the gospel of Jesus Christ can restore people to a right relationship with their Creator. Only the loving grace of God can transform our selfishness into faithfulness. A self-centered life can be turned around to become a God-centered life on mission.

But this mission isn't something we do for God.

It's God's mission.

That mission is the work God has been doing since the beginning of time. The mission of God requires that His people leverage their lives for His glory, using their time, influence, and abilities to share the good news of salvation. Before ascending to heaven, Jesus called His disciples to join this work:

Jesus came near and said to them, "All authority has been given to Me in heaven and on earth. Go, therefore, and make disciples of all nations, baptizing them in the name of the Father and of the Son and of the Holy Spirit, teaching them to observe everything I have commanded you. And remember, I am with you always, to the end of the age."

MATTHEW 28:18-20

The Great Commission isn't for a select few; it's for everyone who follows Christ. The movement of God's mission sweeps across everyday, ordinary lives to draw in businesspeople, soccer moms, grandmothers, neighbors, students, lawyers, teachers, baristas, contractors, white collar, blue collar, or no collar at all. God's mission goes forward through the work of regular people like you and me, filled with the Spirit, laying down our lives, denying ourselves for the mission of God and the redemption of sinful people. This is the invitation.

Jesus invited us to life on mission
over two thousand years ago.

It's not a program or a method of evangelism.
It's the movement of God.

Through His church—all God's people.
This is God's plan to change the world.

LIFE ON MISSION

Many people believe mission and ministry are carried out by a select few professional clergy or an elite number of mission agencies and nonprofit organizations. But in reality, God's mission was given to every member of His church. All Christ followers are called to be everyday missionaries.

Everyday missionaries practice life on mission where God has placed them, whether in an office complex, a Third World country, or a college campus. For the mission to reach fulfillment, every believer must participate willingly, passionately, and sacrificially.

Ephesians 4 tells us God has given leaders to the church to build up His people until they "become mature, attaining to the whole measure of the fullness of Christ" (Eph. 4:13, NIV). That verse doesn't say church leaders are placed over us to do all the work. When we choose to join God on His mission through His church, we dare to be the everyday missionaries He called us to be, to carry out the work of the gospel.

Your life has a mission. If you're a follower of Jesus, He has a purpose and a plan for you. Ephesians 3:20 tells us God is able "to do far more abundantly beyond all that we ask or think, according to the power that works within us" (NASB). Think about that: the God of the universe has a plan far beyond what your mind can conceive. He wants to do more in and through you than you can imagine. What exactly does that look like? What does that mean? How will it all play out in the coming weeks and in the next five years?

We live in a culture that's all about us. Social media has ushered in the selfie generation, which defines itself by self-promotion. In contrast, the purpose of God's mission isn't about us. As we begin to understand what life on mission is about, it's vital to understand our goals. The ultimate goal isn't for us to do good things for others. It's not even to start churches or share our faith. Yes, those are good aspects of the mission, but they aren't the ultimate aim. The ultimate aim of our lives is to bring glory to God.

Ephesians 3:21 identifies the central purpose of any effort we give to God's mission: "To him be glory in the church and in Christ Jesus throughout all generations, forever and ever" (ESV). One early church document tells us, "Man's chief and highest end is to glorify God, and fully to enjoy him forever."[1] The goal of the mission is God's glory.

You don't have to waste years of your life wondering what your purpose is. First Corinthians 10:31 says, "Whether you eat or drink, or whatever you do, do everything for God's glory." The purpose of your parenting is to glorify God. The purpose of your job is to glorify God. And the purpose of your life's mission is to glorify God.

Maybe you think, *OK, I get it. Living for God's glory is the aim, and joining God in His mission to reach my community and beyond is a means toward that great intention, but I have no idea how I'm going to add missions to the chaos called my life.*

The objective of this study isn't to get you involved in some new missions program or create another church event but rather to walk alongside you in creating gospel intentionality within the everyday rhythms of your life. We want to help you have conversations in your everyday life that share the transformative hope and power of the gospel.

The approach we'll share is as simple as 1-2-3. Three Circles is a simple way to share your faith as you focus on these key truths:

God's design

Brokenness

Gospel

By the end of this study, you should be comfortable introducing Three Circles in daily conversations with other people. The Three Circles diagram and easy-to-remember concepts provide a natural way to share the good news of Jesus with the lost people you encounter every day.

---

1. "Westminster Larger Catechism" [online, cited 6 August 2014]. Available from the Internet: *www.reformed.org/documents.*

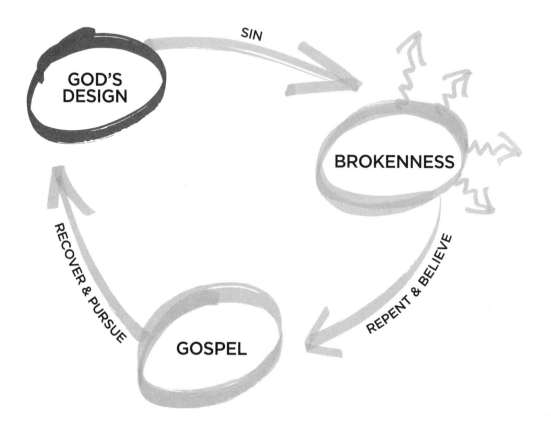

The Bible tells us that God originally designed a world that worked perfectly, where everything and everyone fit together in harmony. God made each of us with a purpose: to worship Him and walk with Him.

GOD'S DESIGN

God's perfect design echoes in His creation. The world God created is so intricate and so detailed that His perfect design is obvious. The best argument for God's design is the presence of life and the beauty of creation.

A few key threads run through this week's personal study on God's design:

1. God's plan is truly good.

2. God Himself is holy and good.

3. Although sin marred God's creation, it couldn't thwart His plans. He will prevail. When God wins, we win too. Part of the perfection of God's plan is the forgiveness of human sins and the access forgiven people have to a restored relationship with our Creator.

Human sin marred God's perfect design for creation. Life on mission can't be lived without an understanding of both God's undeniable goodness and of humanity's overwhelming brokenness. Jesus' sacrifice wasn't a desperate plan B to fix what went wrong in creation. It was God's perfect plan to declare His perfect goodness against all odds.

As people saved by God's grace, we long for the completion of God's perfect plan and the unfolding of His original design of perfect relationship with His creation. Longing for the restoration of God's original design means being part of His redemptive plan. It means pointing others to it as well.

DAY 1
IT WAS GOOD

Genesis 1 shows us the way God's creation was originally intended to function.

Read Genesis 1:27-31. What part of creation most clearly speaks to you about God's perfect design?

People were created in the image of God. Therefore, His handiwork could be seen most vividly through the humans who bore his likeness. The earth was theirs to own and rule. All vegetation was theirs for substance and provision. Everything worked, and everything worked together. God took a careful survey of it all and declared it good (see v. 31).

There's no way to deny that God's creation is good. In spite of sin, people are still made in the image of a loving Creator. Long after sin entered the world, David wrote that the skies and heavens reveal God's glory and pronounce His fame:

> The heavens declare the glory of God,
> and the sky proclaims the work of His hands.
> **PSALM 19:1**

Even in a world corrupted by sin, God makes Himself and His ways known.

Describe what perfect communion with God would be like.

In what ways is creation out of sync with God's original design?

Read Psalm 33:11.

> The counsel of the LORD stands forever,
> the plans of His heart from generation to generation.
> **PSALM 33:11**

What does this verse indicate about God's design?

What does Psalm 33:11 mean for a follower of Jesus?

God's design not only speaks to believers but can also benefit unbelievers. Creation points to the goodness of God and to His reality as the Creator of life. God's good creation points unbelievers to His love and power.

Creation, through the power of the Holy Spirit, can also lead an unbeliever to conviction. God's Word and God's people serve as lights to an unbelieving world when they live a life that gives evidence of His plan.

When an unbeliever denies God because of the current brokenness of the world, you can redirect the conversation toward God's good design and toward His ultimate goal to restore creation. That's a necessary step in faith sharing. Without an understanding of brokenness, people don't comprehend sin. Without an understanding of God's design, people can't imagine salvation.

When you encounter brokenness in the world this week, look for ways to expose the beauty of God's design.

DAY 2
HIGHLIGHTING GOD'S CHARACTER

Part of recognizing and celebrating God's good design is acknowledging the greatness, majesty, and wisdom of God Himself. He has told us:

> "My thoughts are not your thoughts,
> and your ways are not My ways."
> This is the LORD's declaration.
> "For as heaven is higher than earth,
> so My ways are higher than your ways,
> and My thoughts than your thoughts.
> For just as rain and snow fall from heaven
> and do not return there
> without saturating the earth
> and making it germinate and sprout,
> and providing seed to sow
> and food to eat,
> so My word that comes from My mouth
> will not return to Me empty,
> but it will accomplish what I please
> and will prosper in what I send it to do."
> **ISAIAH 55:8-11**

God's attributes are endless. He's completely supreme yet personal and intimate. He's wholly beyond us and impossible for us to completely comprehend, yet He reveals Himself to us and makes Himself knowable. He's never early or late but always exactly on time. He's complete love yet justifiable in His holy wrath.

List as many of God's attributes as you can name.

Which of these attributes do you need most right now?

Describe a time when you learned to trust God more because of one of His particular character traits.

As you prepare to invest your life in unbelievers, focus on attributes of God that you can share. The following activities will help you expand your personal testimony and develop conversation points.

Read 1 John 4:7-10. Describe a time when God personally revealed His love to you.

Read James 1:17. Provide an example of God's ongoing generosity in your life.

Review Isaiah 55:8-11. Describe a time when God's plans were better than your plans.

How can sharing one or more of these experiences help you influence someone for Christ?

When you consider God's character, you discover a treasure trove of opportunities to share stories of His faithfulness in your life. You can communicate to unbelievers how He has shown you love or care, how He has illustrated His sovereignty and demonstrated His power, and how He has proved His plans and provided daily resources. These are all testimonies you can tell and opportunities you can seize to show someone the nature of God and His good design for relating to all who open their hearts to Him.

Review the list you composed of God's attributes. Begin to consider the personal ways He has offered you those parts of His character. Develop an inventory of stories you can share to point others to God's goodness in your life.

DAY 3
WHAT HAPPENED?

What happened to God's perfect world? As the account of Adam and Eve shows, life doesn't work when we ignore God and His original design for our lives. We selfishly insist on doing things our own way. The Bible calls this sin. We all sin and distort the original design:

> They exchanged the truth of God for a lie,
> and worshiped and served something created
> instead of the Creator, who is praised forever.
> **ROMANS 1:25**

Human beings represent a vibrant array of human differences, all highlighting God's overwhelming creativity in the world. Yet we have one dark commonality: sin. Sin is universal when it comes to describing humankind:

> All have sinned and fall short of the glory of God.
> **ROMANS 3:23**

Simply put, sin is going our own way. It includes words, thoughts, actions, and attitudes that separate us from Holy God. It's the natural tendency of people to sin because our very nature is sinful. The consequence of our sin is separation from God—in this life and for all eternity.

Sin is also the most necessary component of a theological understanding of grace and salvation. Without comprehending sin, people can't recognize a need for grace. Without admitting sin, there's no opportunity for salvation. Sin keeps us from God; it's the reason we need Jesus:

> The wages of sin is death, but the gift of God
> is eternal life in Christ Jesus our Lord.
> **ROMANS 6:23**

Read 1 John 1:8,10. How did you first realize that you were a sinner?

Why is recognizing sin such an important component of grasping the goodness of God's salvation?

Identify people in your life who refuse to believe in human sinfulness.

What do you perceive as the barriers between these people and an accurate picture of their sin?

Having a conversation about sin without pointing fingers is a challenge. Avoiding that conversation for fear of alienating or offending someone is understandable, but it isn't the most compassionate course. If the effort to keep peace limits the acceptance of an essential spiritual truth, we're faced with a risk worth taking. The apostle Paul admonishes us to speak "the truth in love" (Eph. 4:15). When we attempt to do that in the context of a relationship we've invested ourselves in, we earn the right to be heard and lessen the potential of alienating the person.

If we genuinely care about someone's eternal destiny, we can't bypass the danger of sin. It's because of sin's dark curse that we can truly revel in God's great gift. It's a tough topic but one that must be addressed. The goal isn't to condemn but to reveal God's plan for our redemption. Recognizing sin emphasizes the good news of a God who has made a way for us to experience the joy of His salvation.

Ask God to equip you with a Spirit-filled gentleness when talking about sin so that the people in your life who need salvation will be drawn closer to Jesus.

DAY 4
RELATIONSHIP

When Jesus went to Zacchaeus's home, it was scandalous (see Luke 19:1-10). To share a meal in someone's home indicated intimacy. It illustrated relationship. Everyone knew a tax collector had no business being seen with the Savior.

What they didn't understand was the hope available to sinners. Jesus may have been too good for Zacchaeus, but Zacchaeus wasn't too bad for Jesus. Zacchaeus could have never worked his way into God's favor. But his sin didn't mean he was in no position to receive it. That's why we call grace God's unmerited favor.

Did you ever consider your lostness beyond God's grasp or Christ's love? Why or why not?

How have you personally experienced hospitality and communion with Christ?

Identify types of people who parallel the tax collector in this account.

How can you emulate the actions of Christ when relating to the tax collectors of the world?

What will your willingness to be hospitable toward fellow sinners communicate to them about a restored relationship with God through Jesus?

As the apostle Paul wrote, our ability to enter a relationship with God through the gospel has nothing to do with our works and everything to do with God's grace. God gives grace so that we can be in a relationship with Him. It's part of His divine design-restoration plan:

> Don't be ashamed of the testimony about our Lord,
>   or of me His prisoner. Instead, share in suffering
>   for the gospel, relying on the power of God.
> He has saved us and called us
> with a holy calling,
> not according to our works,
> but according to His own purpose and grace,
> which was given to us in Christ Jesus
> before time began.
> **2 TIMOTHY 1:8-9**

How is the willingness to suffer for the sake of the gospel (see v. 8) evidence of a relationship with Christ?

Describe a time when you suffered for the sake of communicating the gospel. Did you feel closer to Christ in that moment or farther away?

How can your willingness to share in Christ's suffering clear up any confusion about what it means to follow Him?

Rather than seeing God's power as a "Get out of suffering free" card, we should perceive it as a "Get through suffering" guarantee card. Although getting through suffering doesn't come without pain and consequences, it yields a testimony of either God's rescue or God's sustaining. Ultimately, walking through pain and rejection helps us identify with Jesus' passionate sacrifice. You're among those whom Christ came to seek and save. And He suffered immensely for it.

Seize moments to speak of your relationship with God in your interactions with others. Show them firsthand how God reached out to you and how a relationship with Him has affected your life.

DAY 5
GOD'S DESIGN RESTORED

No one knows exactly what heaven and the afterlife will really be like, but Scripture offers us several certainties:

1. Believers will be with Christ.

2. Not everyone will enter.

Jesus said in Matthew 7:

> Enter through the narrow gate. For the gate is wide and the road is broad that leads to destruction, and there are many who go through it. How narrow is the gate and difficult the road that leads to life, and few find it. Not everyone who says to Me, "Lord, Lord!" will enter the kingdom of heaven, but only the one who does the will of My Father in heaven.
> **MATTHEW 7:13-14,21**

When it comes to eternity, it's easy to confess among a group of like-minded Christians your understanding of who will spend eternity with God. After all, like you, they believe in Jesus. The only requirement is belief. God designed an eternity package full of rich covenant blessings, and the part of the equation you bring to the table is belief. Try having that conversation with someone who doesn't believe, and you're suddenly labeled an intolerant subhuman. Instinctively, you might be tempted to back down from your convictions about what God's Word really says.

How can we make sure we're true believers? Paul gave us this clue:

> If you have been raised with the Messiah, seek what is above, where the Messiah is, seated at the right hand of God. Set your minds on what is above, not on what is on the earth. For you have died, and your life is hidden with the Messiah in God. When the Messiah, who is your life, is revealed, then you also will be revealed with Him in glory.
>
> **COLOSSIANS 3:1-4**

Paul could have written that the Messiah is your Savior. Instead, he said the Messiah is your life. That's because the kind of belief Scripture requires is total, life-changing belief. According to James 2:19, even demons believe. The problem is that their belief doesn't lead them to submit to the authority of God and trust Him only. It's not a life-changing belief. In Matthew 7 Jesus said the gate is narrow. Not everyone who professes to believe in Him will experience His perfect eternity. Why? Theirs isn't a life-changing belief.

> *How would you describe life-changing belief as opposed to simple acknowledgment of who Jesus is?*

> *What indicator does Jesus give at the end of Matthew 7:21 to show us what life-changing belief looks like?*

In John 14:1-4 Jesus told His disciples that He would ascend into heaven, where He's now busy preparing a place for us and all believers. In other words, Jesus is restoring God's design. Ultimately, Jesus will bring about the perfect, permanent communal relationship between God and His children.

> *How does knowing your ultimate destiny motivate your life-on-mission efforts?*

Think about heaven this week. Let God's promise to restore His relational design between Himself and His creation motivate you to reach out to others who need to know Him. Be willing to enter conversations in which you might be required to stand by the conviction that only believers will experience that restored eternity. Also make certain your relationship with Christ aligns with what Scripture teaches about life-changing belief. Simple acknowledgment of Jesus isn't enough.

SESSION 2

START

Start the group session by having everyone respond to one of the following questions.

What's the greatest experience of your life?
OR
What's the most beautiful place you've ever been?

After everyone has had a chance to respond, follow up by asking this question.

What made that experience or place so amazing?

Transition to the video with the following thought.

We all have moments when things feel right and good. Something inside us recognizes that there's more to life than our ordinary experience. In today's session we'll discuss God's original design and intention for our lives.

Videos available for purchase at
www.lifeway.com/lifeonmission

WATCH

Follow the notes below as you watch this week's video featuring Ellis Prince.

- • God's design is birthed out of relationship.

- • Jesus died so we could be a family.

- • God's design is selflessness. The world is selfish.

- • You represent a family. The end result of the gospel is an expanded family.

- • When you live your life on display, people are going to initiate the conversation with you. When they initiate it, they're ready to hear what you have to say.

- • Ask God's Spirit who, when, and how to begin to talk to people.

- • If you do not share a personal story of interaction with God, your evangelism is going to fall short.

Scripture references: Genesis 3:8; John 13:35; 1 Peter 3:15; Colossians 3:5-14; Galatians 5:19-23; Luke 15:4-6

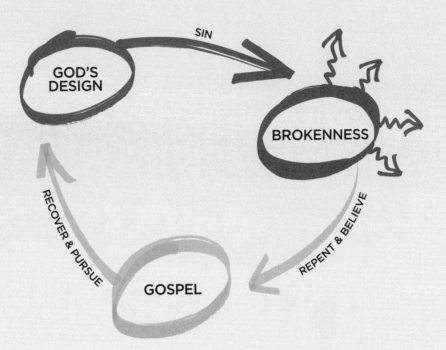

RESPOND

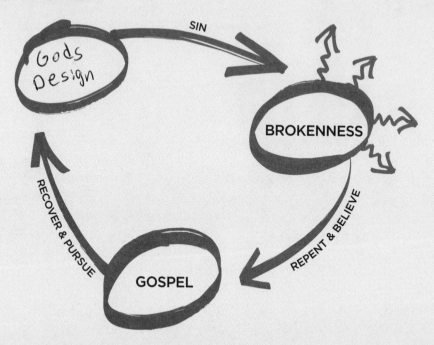

Begin the response time by filling in the missing words above. (The diagram in each session will build on the previous one.) Ask a volunteer to share the answer.

Ask two people to read aloud Genesis 1:31 and Psalm 19:1. (See day 1.)

How would you describe God's design for all creation?

Ask three people to read aloud John 13:35; Colossians 3:12-14; Galatians 5:22-23.

What is God's design for us?

Love one another

In the video Ellis said, "God's design is birthed out of relationship," and we "represent a family." What does that mean? (See days 4–5.)

How would you briefly explain the meaning of the first circle representing God's design?

GOD'S DESIGN

How would you introduce a discussion about God's design in a conversation? What could you point to in nature or in daily life to direct the conversation toward God and His design?

Genus ③

If God's design was perfect, what happened? Why isn't perfection our daily experience? (See day 3.)

Conversations often start with brokenness—hardship, pain, and suffering. In the next session we'll learn how to make the transition from relating to someone's experience of brokenness to sharing the hope of God's perfect design.

How would you contrast the beauty of God's design with the current brokenness of the fallen world?

In what ways do you see people longing for God's design but not necessarily recognizing that hunger?

Finally, in the video Ellis emphasized the need to share our experiences.

How did you come to understand God's design for your life?

How can the church—all God's people—experience more of God by fully embracing His design for life on mission? (See day 2.)

Wrap up the session with any final questions or observations before closing with prayer. Thank God for His glorious design. Ask God's Spirit who, when, and how to begin talking to people who need to know God's perfect plan for them.

Use the next page to record ideas, questions, or prayers.

Complete the personal study in "Brokenness" before the next group session.

PERSONAL STUDY

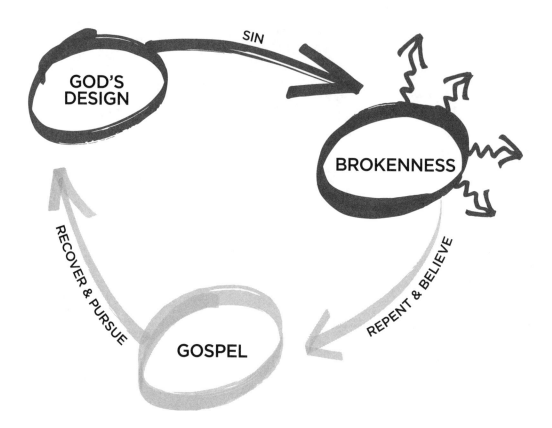

So what happened to God's perfect world? Wanting to be in charge, humans rejected God and His original design. The Bible calls this sin. Like a virus, sin is passed down from generation to generation, distorting God's original design. The consequences of sin are brokenness and separation from God.

BROKENNESS

Where do you see brokenness in your life? In your family? In your community? In your workplace?

Three simple truths about brokenness are presented in this week's study:

1. The world is broken.

2. No one can completely escape the effects of brokenness.

3. Everyone endures hardships caused by brokenness, and everyone contributes to the brokenness of the world.

In the middle of a broken world, how do you relate to others and point them to hope and a solution? After all, you're broken too.

As those who have been rescued and are being transformed by Jesus Christ, we know that hope is found only in Him. Nothing in this world will satisfy. Our mission is driven by the truth of the gospel and is defined by the redemptive plan of God. God's mission is to take what's broken and redeem it—not simply to make it better but to make it new. And the exciting part is that God Himself invites us to follow Him into a broken world as we live life on mission.

DAY 1
THE WORLD
IS BROKEN

Brokenness is a reality in this life. War. Natural disaster. Persecution. Violence. Hatred. Abuse. Deception. Corruption. Crime. Physical, emotional, mental, and spiritual exhaustion. Disease and death.

There's no way to deny that the world we live in is broken. Seriously, desperately broken. But there's hope. The good news of God's kingdom—the gospel of Jesus—will be taken to broken people in every part of this broken world before it all falls apart.

Jesus promised His disciples that the world would become a lot worse before it got better.

Read Matthew 24:6-14. What kinds of brokenness did Jesus identify?

God has invited you to join His mission. The "good news of the kingdom will be proclaimed in all the whole world" (Matt. 24:14) by people like you and me. We participate in His mission by sharing the gospel—the good news—with broken people who need God's grace. The good news of His kingdom will spread throughout the world. And no matter how dark and bleak things may get, this mission will not fail.

What's a recent example of the world's brokenness in the news or in your own life?

What's the biggest example of the world's brokenness you've personally experienced?

Consider the community around you. What patterns of brokenness characterize your generation?

What burden do you have for your community? For other cultures?

Jesus said our mission to take the good news of His kingdom to people everywhere would succeed, even in the midst of serious problems (see vv. 13-14). What hope does that promise give you?

Think about the people in your neighborhood, at the gym, at school or work, and so on. Whom do you know who has been personally affected by war, natural disaster, crime, abuse, or tragedy? Who has recently suffered from disease or death among loved ones? Write specific names and specific examples of brokenness.

One of the most common conversation pieces is what's wrong in the world. Whether we're speaking with good friends or complete strangers, brokenness naturally surfaces in conversations every day. A cashier or a coworker complains about a tough break. Someone on the elevator comments on the latest headline scrolling on a smartphone. There's no escaping the brokenness of this world. Everyone lives in this reality. Rather than being discouraged or joining the complaints, find hope in Jesus' reassuring words to His followers that life would continue to be hard but that there was a light at the end of this dark tunnel:

> I have told you these things so that in Me you may
> have peace. You will have suffering in this world.
> Be courageous! I have conquered the world.
> **JOHN 16:33**

Be aware of the ways you encounter brokenness this week. Pray that God will open your eyes to suffering. Pray for boldness to share the good news of Christ's kingdom with those you encounter who are dealing with brokenness in their lives.

DAY 2
FAMILIES ARE BROKEN

Every generation is tied to the one before it. This is more than just a genetic code that's passed along from parents to offspring. We all inherit certain traits and tendencies from our families. Everyone is born into a particular culture and circumstance. The Old Testament reminds us that it's easy for a new generation to adopt the sins of the previous one:

> The LORD is slow to anger and rich in faithful love, forgiving wrongdoing and rebellion. But He will not leave the guilty unpunished, bringing the consequences of the fathers' wrongdoing on the children to the third and fourth generation.
> **NUMBERS 14:18**

The people around us are flawed and imperfect, to put it mildly. Unfortunately, some families have long histories of addiction, abuse, crime, racism, or disease. Others seem hopelessly trapped in cycles of poverty, depression, and other overwhelming realities. Nobody chooses the family dynamic they're born into. Nobody chooses their genetic makeup or the environmental factors of their upbringing. No matter how good or bad our families may be on the surface, we were all born into a mess.

In addition, we're all born sinners:

> Just as sin entered the world through one man, and death through sin, in this way death spread to all men, because all sinned.
> **ROMANS 5:12**

These realities don't excuse poor choices, but their impact is undeniable. The world is broken. People are broken, including those in your own family.

Name negative trends in your family history (for example, bad temper, racism, materialism, addiction, laziness, and so forth).

How have patterns from your upbringing surfaced in your own life?

What personal characteristic or behavior (current or past) would you prefer not to pass on to the next generation?

As you look at these lists, confess your sins to God, expressing sorrow and asking for His forgiveness and help.

How has someone ministered to you in dealing with issues you inherited from your family or your upbringing?

Who in your life has been hurt by a broken family or a hard upbringing?

How can you comfort someone who is hurting from family issues?

The fact that the world is broken is a harsh reality. Brokenness in the context of family often inflicts the most painful and shameful wounds in our lives. Many lost people around you—maybe family members—are hurt, and they've inherited hurtful tendencies. These wounds are sensitive, so we need to handle them with care, but they also cause people to be acutely aware of their need for healing. You can be ready to introduce them to the One who can heal their wounds.

Pray for an awareness of your own inherited sinfulness and for sensitivity to the deep wounds in your family. Begin praying for God's supernatural healing and the freedom that's found only in Jesus.

DAY 3
YOU ARE BROKEN

No one's perfect, right? People say this all the time, and it's true. But it's not an excuse. The phrase is rarely used to make a confession or assume responsibility. People tend to respond to the brokenness of the world in two ways:

1. Rationalizing sin

2. Minimizing sin

Yes, the world is broken. Yes, your family is broken. Yes, you inherited a mess. And yes, you're broken. But you must own your part in the problem. You are personally responsible for your part of the mess. This is true in society and before God. No amount of rationalizing or minimizing on your part can change that.

Through the prophet Jeremiah, God declared that He holds each of us responsible for our own sin:

> In those days, it will never again be said:
> The fathers have eaten sour grapes,
> and the children's teeth are set on edge.
> Rather, each will die for his own wrongdoing. Anyone
> who eats sour grapes—his own teeth will be set on edge.
> **JEREMIAH 31:29-30**

What sins have you tried to excuse with statements like "It's just the way I am" or "I can't help it"?

In what ways do you see your culture avoiding personal responsibility?

Identify areas of your life where you still struggle with brokenness.

Read Psalm 51:5-10. What words indicate that David took responsibility for his sin?

How can you gently bring up personal ownership of brokenness to a friend who is blaming someone or something else?

How would you explain the hope and healing that come from recognizing your own brokenness?

You're broken. We all are. But don't let "We're all broken" be an excuse to avoid the problem. Let it be permission to deal with your problem. Admit it. Own it. But don't settle for it. Like the psalmist, cry out to God for a better reality. Crave healing, wholeness, and freedom. Admitting guilt is the first step in dealing with the problem. Just as you can't be healed if you won't admit you're sick, brokenness can't be fixed if you won't admit you're broken.

Confess your brokenness before God and ask for healing. Also pray for the humility to confess your need for healing to others, thereby disarming their defenses and inviting them to recognize and confess their own brokenness.

DAY 4
DEALING WITH HURT

Here are two facts of life you can always count on:

1. People will hurt you.

2. People around you are hurting.

And for anyone who joins the mission of God as a follower of Jesus, there are two simple responses to these realities:

1. When people hurt you, turn the other cheek (see Luke 6:29).

2. When you're around people who are hurting, weep with those who weep (see Rom. 12:15).

Warning: these actions may sound simple, but neither is easy. Natural human desire is often the exact opposite of these biblical ideals.

When someone hurts you, it's a symptom of brokenness. The only cure is to offer a remedy to the real problem. Lashing out may scratch the itch for a moment, but it does nothing to heal the issue. In fact, fighting back will not only make your own problem worse but will also push that person further away from the hope of healing you have as a child of the Heavenly Father.

Hurting people need to be fixed. You can't fix yourself, and you can't fix the other person. Your best move is to point them to Jesus, the only One who can fix you both.

Your mission is to share the good news. You're to spend your life showing people the life and love of Jesus.

When has someone knowingly done something to hurt you or take advantage of you? How did you respond?

Did your response help or hurt your situation?

How did your response affect that person's ability to see Jesus in you?

In your life right now, how can you turn the other cheek in order to show someone the humble love of Jesus?

Sometimes we aren't directly involved in pain or conflict. When people around us are hurting, the first thing to do is sympathize with the hurting. People aren't always ready for a theological discussion or practical advice. Sometimes all they need is to know we care. They might just need a shoulder or a listening ear. They might just need us to be there. Presence is a powerful ministry.

Who in your life is dealing with an unfair or painful situation?

How can you intentionally provide presence or comfort?

God can use quiet moments of weeping with those who weep as a testimony that people will never forget. The world is quick to demand or to give advice. Often children of God can best show Jesus' love by humbly being present and by loving and listening to neighbors and enemies alike.

Pray for humility, trusting God to provide opportunities to talk about His love and opportunities to model it in selfless actions. Seize moments to turn the other cheek, listen, weep, and comfort.

DAY 5
PURE AND UNDEFILED

Life on mission isn't based on convenience or directed only toward people who are like you. The Bible reveals that God is deeply concerned for the poor and the outcast, those who are helpless and on the fringes of society. Often these include orphans and widows who are unable to adequately provide for their needs. James described a believer's responsibility for these people:

> Pure and undefiled religion before our God and Father
> is this: to look after orphans and widows in their distress
> and to keep oneself unstained by the world.
> **JAMES 1:27**

In our society, one that's driven by comfort and success, James's teaching is shockingly countercultural. Many people think of religion as something learned, earned, or achieved. But Scripture is clear that good doctrine and morals aren't the defining characteristics of God's family. God expects His children to express their religious convictions in compassionate acts of ministry, loving the unlovely and caring for those who can't care for themselves.

This ministry isn't easy or convenient. It requires going out of our way, perhaps entering other parts of town that make us uncomfortable. Jesus told two sobering parables about loving people in need. In one story an unexpected hero, commonly known as the good Samaritan, abandons his schedule to care for a man in need (see Luke 10:25-37). In another parable Jesus separates sheep and goats and distributes eternal reward or judgment based on the way they care for the sick, imprisoned, and needy children of God (see Matt. 25:31-46).

In the first parable Jesus made it painfully clear that the people who are typically recognized as religious fail to love their neighbors and consequently fail to love Him. People who go out of their way to love "the least of these brothers of Mine"

(Matt. 25:40) demonstrate the love that a broken world so desperately needs. Those people enjoy eternal life with Jesus.

Who in your life is hardest to love?

Where do you tend to avoid people in your community?

Who are "the least of these" in your community?

Make a list of your daily activities. Do you spend most or all of your time in places comfortable to you and with people like you?

What can you do to intentionally show love to broken and needy people?

Today's lesson isn't intended to make you feel guilty or to manipulate you to perform a service project. It's natural for people to gravitate toward people like themselves. It's also natural for people to spend time with people who are self-sufficient or who can benefit them in some way. But when we follow Christ and cultivate a heart like His, it should become equally natural for us to extend the love we've received to those in obvious need.

Sometimes when lost people seem to have it all together on the surface, it's difficult to admit their brokenness and their need for God. But when they have obvious needs, they're most open to and grateful for help and hope. Pray for God to open your eyes and direct your steps to those in need. Pray for selfless compassion toward the hurting, broken people around you and be ready to offer the eternal solutions that only God can provide.

Discover opportunities to go out of your way to care for widows, orphans, the sick, the imprisoned, the hungry, or the hurting. What spiritual needs are evident in these situations? Make notes about your experience.

SESSION 3

START

Start the group session with the following question.

> *If you could end or prevent one injustice, tragedy, or problem in the world today, what would it be? Why?*

> *(There are no right or wrong answers.)*

After everyone has had a chance to respond, follow up by asking these questions.

> *What does the existence of problems and suffering tell us about the world?*

> *What does your desire to fix the problem you identified tell you about the way God made you?*

Transition to the video with the following thought.

The world is full of pain and hardship; everybody knows this. In the previous session we started by identifying moments when things felt right and good. But we can't escape the reality that things often go wrong and bad things keep happening. In today's session we'll discuss the brokenness that characterizes the world.

BROKENNESS

WATCH

Follow the notes below as you watch this week's video featuring Eric Mason.

- Everybody has a level of brokenness.

- Christ has dealt with our brokenness, is dealing with our brokenness, and will ultimately remove it.

- Two types of brokenness: brokenness from personal sin and brokenness from living on a broken planet

- The purpose of brokenness in unbelievers is to open people up.

- The purpose of brokenness in believers is to show the treasure.

- Jesus is the center of the church.

Scripture references: Psalms 34; 51; 2 Corinthians 4:7-11; 2 Corinthians 11:22-27; Mark 7:25-30; Genesis 32:24-30; Genesis 1–3

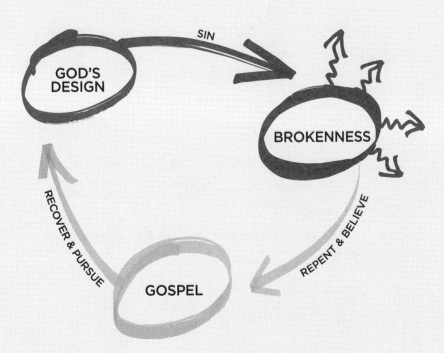

RESPOND

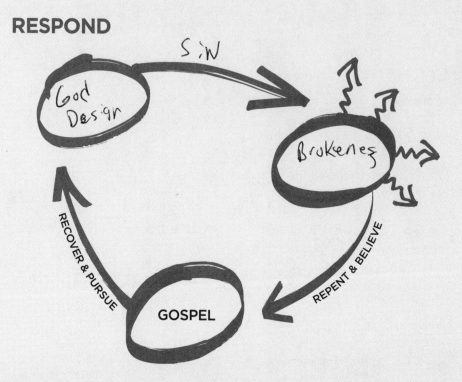

Begin the response time by filling in the missing words above. Ask a volunteer to share the answers, reviewing what was discussed in the previous session.

How did we get from God's perfect design to our current reality of brokenness?

Ask two people to read aloud Matthew 24:6-14; Romans 3:10-18.

How would you explain brokenness and a fallen world?

What evidence of human brokenness do you see in the world today? (See days 1–2.)

BROKENNESS

Eric mentioned two types of brokenness: brokenness from personal sin and brokenness from living on a broken planet.

How have you experienced each type of brokenness? (See day 3.)

How did the pain of brokenness and the hard questions about brokenness awaken you to your need for God?

How is brokenness often a natural starting point for conversations about God's design and ultimately the gospel?

When has God used you to comfort others in the middle of their brokenness? (See days 3–4.)

How has God used the brokennness in your life to show His love to others?

Who are the broken and needy people around you? How can you be intentional about showing the love of God to them? (See day 5.)

Wrap up the session with any final questions or observations. Read Psalm 51 aloud as a closing prayer, pausing for a brief moment after each verse to allow personal reflection by everyone in the group.

Use the next page to record ideas, questions, or prayers.

Complete the personal study in "Gospel" before the next group session.

PERSONAL STUDY

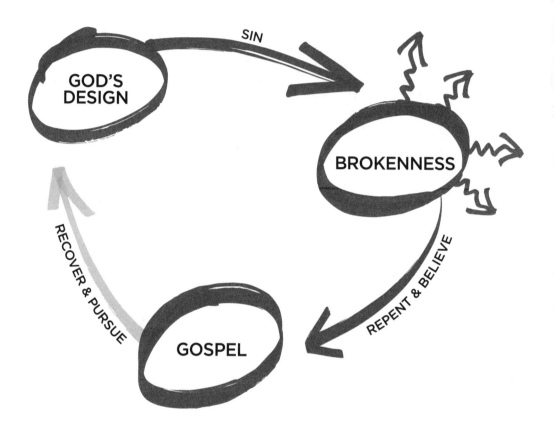

God didn't leave us in our brokenness. Jesus, God in human flesh, came to us and lived perfectly according to God's design. He took our sin and shame to the cross, dying to pay the penalty for our separation. He was then raised from the dead to provide the only way for us to be rescued and restored to a relationship with God. This is the good news. This is the gospel.

GOSPEL

Think of the last time you were ill and went to the local pharmacy for an over-the-counter remedy. Your symptoms, whether a runny nose or a cough, gave you clues about the cause of your illness. Similarly, brokenness in the world is a symptom of a horrible disease called sin. The condition of all humankind is desperate brokenness in search of the right remedy. There are countless options, all making incredible promises, but only one absolute cure.

That cure is the gospel—the good news of Jesus. While all things and circumstances won't become immediately perfect in this world, our brokenness is forever healed by the message of hope found in Christ. What good works, effort, will, and desire could never accomplish, God freely gave through the death, burial, and resurrection of His Son. Each component of salvation's protocol is essential. Sin demanded death. Death had to be defeated. Resurrection had to be real for salvation to be bought. And glorious restoration is made possible for sinners.

Living life on mission means advancing that gospel message. The world may be knocking down death's door, but a remedy is available. The gospel doesn't just mask symptoms. It cures the disease.

DAY 1
HELP NEEDED

There are many differences between Christianity and other major world religions. Perhaps the greatest is the Christian understanding of grace. Other religions might be characterized as "do" plans requiring adherents to complete certain tasks or behave in certain ways to earn or keep eternal life. Christianity can be summed up as a "done" plan because all that's required in salvation for a Christ follower has been done. The physical purchase of freedom was made with Christ's blood (see John 3:16; Col. 2:14).

While it's easy to get tripped up and live life under the fear or threat of earning or losing God's favor, we must constantly be reminded that any self-effort to escape the trap of brokenness is futile. Salvation is a free gift of God's grace:

> You are saved by grace through faith, and this
> is not from yourselves; it is God's gift—not
> from works, so that no one can boast.
> **EPHESIANS 2:8-9**

What are some practices or traditions people in the world might assume are requirements of salvation in Christianity?

How have you dealt with the pressure to earn or maintain salvation through performance or behavioral change?

In spite of the impression that salvation can be earned, the truth is that sin has overtaken all people, and there's nothing they can do to slow its harmful effects and its inevitable victory. Sin demands death, and that demand must be met. The good news is that our Heavenly Father, in His great love, has offered an atoning sacrifice for the sins of the world (see 1 John 2:2).

Simply hearing this good news isn't enough. People must admit their sinful brokenness and stop trusting in themselves. They don't have the power to escape this brokenness on their own. They need to be rescued.

How do you introduce Jesus' crucifixion and resurrection in spiritual conversations?

If you don't reach the point of introducing Jesus' death and resurrection to other people, what are the reasons?

Read John 3:16. What was the motivation behind God's great gift of His Son for our sin?

Read John 14:6-7. What was the method of God's redemptive plan?

Some people take exception to the Bible's assertion that Jesus is the only way to be saved. But the gospel, the good news, is that salvation is available to all who believe. All sinners' debts can be erased, and all sinners can be fully known and made fully alive in Christ. Live your life on mission so that the broken people you know can hear and respond to the gospel.

Identify a relationship you have with someone who is broken and is ready to hear the gospel. Outline a way you could introduce the gospel in a conversation with that person. Then create an opportunity to dive into the spiritual conversation.

DAY 2
GOOD NEWS

The word *gospel* means *good news.* That's easy enough to understand. The gospel is all-encompassing. It reaches every facet of our being and leaves nothing untouched. It transforms the very fabric of our lives.

> *Read 1 Corinthians 15:3-4 and list the essential components of the gospel message.*

> *What's your understanding of the meaning of the gospel?*

John the Baptist heralded the good news of Jesus' coming by telling people that the kingdom of God had arrived. It was great news to a community of people longing for a new government. But that would have been only a temporary fix until the next time people disobeyed and God allowed another hostile takeover of Israel. In contrast to the people's expectations, Jesus ushered in a kingdom that couldn't be moved (see Heb. 12:28).

The kingdom of God is a gospel message. It offers people a way to live above and beyond culture and provides an opportunity for every part of life to be completely transformed for God's purposes and glory. The gospel isn't about what's coming. The gospel is about who came and who is here—the Savior who promised:

> I am the door. If anyone enters by Me, he will be saved and will come in and go out and find pasture. A thief comes only to steal and to kill and to destroy. I have come so that they may have life and have it in abundance.
> **JOHN 10:9-10**

Briefly describe your life before Christ. If you became a Christ follower at a young age, describe a time in your life when you didn't follow Jesus faithfully. This is your pretransformation life.

Name an area of your life on which the gospel has made a tremendous impact. Describe the transformation you experienced.

What do you think it means to live an abundant life in Christ?

How would you describe the abundant life to someone else?

The gospel is not only the story of Christ and His sacrifice but also the transformed testimony of a believer in Jesus. You can't have one without the other. When we share the gospel, we need to communicate the gospel definition outlining Jesus' life and ministry, as well as a definition of God's power made alive in a believer today. Presentations of Christ's sacrificial act and testimonies about the fullness of life he affords believers today demonstrate the power of the kingdom that's available to all who believe.

Be sure to understand both parts of a good gospel presentation: the sacrifice of Jesus and the way He's changed your life. Pray and ask God to give you noticeable moments to share each part of the story.

DAY 3 REPENT AND BELIEVE

When presented with the gospel message, what must sinners do to be saved? The Gospel of Mark tells us:

> After John was arrested, Jesus went to Galilee, preaching the good news of God: "The time is fulfilled, and the kingdom of God has come near. Repent and believe in the good news!"
>
> **MARK 1:14-15**

People must ask God to forgive them, turning from sin to trust only in Jesus. This is what it means to repent and believe. Repentance is the idea of turning from sin and turning to Christ. It's the action that follows from belief. Repentance shouldn't be equated with work. Salvation isn't based on what we do but on the transformation that God brings about in our hearts through grace (see Eph. 2:8-9).

When we repent, God turns our lives in a new direction. When we believe God is good, Christ is the true Savior, and forgiveness is free, we wholeheartedly give up our sin and embrace a new way of life. Repentance is the act of desiring God more than sin, His plans more than ours.

Jesus told people to repent and believe the good news because the kingdom of God had come (see Mark 1:15). He was calling us to repent of building our own kingdoms, aligning our lives and our priorities with the kingdom of God.

Describe what repentance looked like when you gave your life to Jesus. How did your thoughts and behavior change?

Compose a sentence of repentance stating what you would say today to indicate an attitude of repentance toward God.

Record the way you would explain repentance with an unbeliever.

When we believe, we receive new life through Jesus. *Believe* is an important word because it describes the way we're saved. The apostle Paul explained:

> If you confess with your mouth, "Jesus is Lord," and believe in your heart that God raised Him from the dead, you will be saved. One believes with the heart, resulting in righteousness, and one confesses with the mouth, resulting in salvation.
> **ROMANS 10:9-10**

For someone who wants to follow Jesus, belief is transformative. It's believing in Jesus and abandoning sin and selfish desires that filter into every area of life. Belief that brings salvation comes from God Himself and changes everything about a person:

> To all who did receive Him, He gave them the right to be children of God, to those who believe in His name.
> **JOHN 1:12**

Ask God to help you reflect the meaning of repentance and belief in the way you live your life in submission to Him and in the way you share the gospel with others. Ask God to identify any area of unconfessed sin you need to repent of and areas of unbelief you need to entrust to Him. Ask Him to guide your discussions of repentance and belief with people who are ready to receive Christ.

DAY 4
PURSUE

Believing in Jesus and experiencing salvation transform every area of life as we pursue Him. Pursuing Jesus—following Him; obeying Him; and allowing Him to transform our mind, behavior, and character—is both a benefit of knowing Christ and a responsibility of walking with Him.

Walking in light of the gospel prompts believers to live a holy life worthy of the calling we've attained. How do we do that? Paul's letter to Rome reminded believers of the importance of being a living sacrifice, one that perpetually honors Christ in response to the mercies they had received:

> Brothers, by the mercies of God, I urge you to present your bodies as a living sacrifice, holy and pleasing to God; this is your spiritual worship. Do not be conformed to this age, but be transformed by the renewing of your mind, so that you may discern what is the good, pleasing, and perfect will of God.
> **ROMANS 12:1-2**

Mercy is God's beautiful act of withholding the punishment for sin we deserve and offering grace instead. Because of that mercy, Paul urged fellow believers to live a transformed life. The evidence of Christ then becomes the method to follow Christ. And this too is one of God's precious gifts to us. All the greatness God requests of us involves tasks He prepared in advance for us to do:

> We are His creation, created in Christ Jesus for good works, which God prepared ahead of time so that we should walk in them.
> **EPHESIANS 2:10**

The faith we have in God is a precious gift from Him. That faith is best illustrated by our worship and our works.

Describe the way you feel most connected to God in worship.

What works do you sense God is calling you to do for Him and through Him?

How would you describe the difference between works done in Christ and works done to try to earn salvation?

How have you been able to discern God's will in your life? Do you find that to be an easy task or a difficult one?

Think about the brokenness in your world, including hurting people you might be called to love, serve, bless, and share Christ with. What works has God prepared in advance for you to do?

How is walking in the works God prepared in advance for you to do an act of worship?

Offering your life to God as a living sacrifice enables you to pursue the holy life He originally designed for all humankind. It also positions you to discern God's will in joining His redemptive mission in the world.

Set aside time to listen to God this week. Ask Him to help you discern His will and walk in His works.

DAY 5
THE GREAT COMMISSION

Living life on mission is incomplete without engaging with two significant passages of Scripture. Matthew 28:18-20, often called the Great Commission, and Acts 1:8 record the final words of Jesus before His ascension into heaven and promise the coming of the indwelling Holy Spirit.

Read Matthew 28:18-20 and Acts 1:8. List features of the verses that are similar and features that are different.

Jesus' Great Commission calls us to make disciples, not converts. What's the difference between converts and disciples?

What insight does each passage provide into the spiritual power God gives us to be on mission?

What are the key parts of the disciple-making strategy provided in Matthew?

Which part of that strategy has come easiest to you? Hardest to you?

How can you apply the strategy for world evangelization provided in Acts?

It's one thing to go on an international mission trip every month and engage the ends of the earth but never take your faith next door. It's another thing to be so consumed with disciple making in your own family that you never engage your neighbor across the street. To fully rest in Christ's power and understand life on mission, we must be engaged in both domestic and international arenas. Every Christian is called to make disciples as we live our life on mission. A Christian is necessarily a missionary in everyday life.

In the past have you been more involved in local or worldwide evangelism? Why?

How can you engage the ends of the earth without ever leaving your locale?

Matthew 28:20 tells us that Jesus will be with us until the end of the age, and Acts 1:8 sends us out to the ends of the earth. Perhaps Christ is delaying the end of the age to allow more time for the mission to be accomplished (see 2 Pet. 3:9). But no matter how far we go or how long we have to spread His name and His fame, we're promised Christ's unlimited power and presence for the mission.

In what way does Jesus' presence make a difference in your response to the Great Commission?

How have you felt or experienced the Holy Spirit's power when sharing your faith? Give a specific example.

Seek the Holy Spirit's power for your spiritual conversations this week. Pray for His guidance in advance and rely on Him to help you make the transition from someone's brokenness to the gospel.

SESSION 4

START

Start the group session with the following questions.

> *What's the biggest relief you've ever felt?*

> *What had you so concerned, and what changed?*

After everyone has had a chance to respond, follow up by asking this question.

> *What did you do after receiving or realizing the good news?*

Transition to the video with the following thought.

When realizing we and our world are broken with sin, we desperately need good news. In today's session we'll discuss the gospel—the most life-changing news in all of history.

WATCH

Follow the notes below as you watch this week's video featuring J. D. Greear.

- The gospel is the good news that God has done everything necessary to save us.

- Repentance means acknowledging that Jesus is the Lord.

- Faith means believing Jesus did what He said He did when He finished the work of our salvation on the cross and embracing that as your own.

- There is no comprehension of the gospel without a comprehension of sin.

- Two prayers: 1. As You have been to me, so I will be to others. 2. I'll measure Your compassion by the cross and Your power by the resurrection.

- Effective evangelists believe two things: 1. Salvation belongs to God. 2. Faith comes only by hearing the word of God (see Rom. 10:17).

Scripture references: Genesis 1–3; John 20:14-17; John 20:22; Exodus 20:3-17; Romans 1:25; Matthew 4:17; Luke 4:18-19,43; Ephesians 5:25; Psalm 126:5; Romans 10:17; Romans 1:16

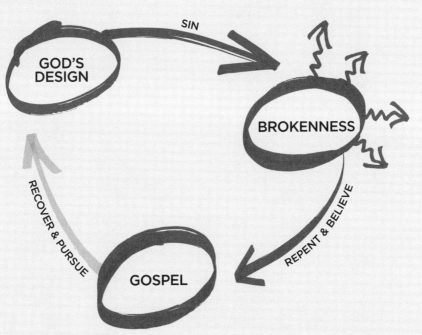

RESPOND

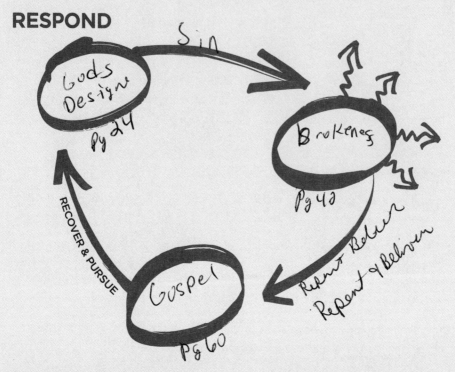

Begin the response time by filling in the missing words above. Then ask a volunteer to share the answers and a brief review of previous concepts.

Why is the gospel truly good news? (See day 2.)

How did we all fall into brokenness, and how do we begin moving out of it? (See day 1.)

Ask three people to read aloud Romans 1:25; 3:23; 6:23.

How would you explain sin to the average person?

J. D. said, "There is no comprehension of the gospel without a comprehension of sin."

What did he mean? Is it possible to share the gospel without discussing sin and repentance, focusing exclusively on belief?

Why do people often avoid talking about sin? (See day 1.)

Ask two people to read aloud John 3:16 and Romans 10:9.

How would you explain repent and believe? (See day 3.)

How would you introduce the gospel, especially in a conversation with a friend who is experiencing brokenness? (See day 5.)

How have you personally been changed by the power of the gospel?

How have you seen the gospel change others?

How does our understanding of the gospel influence our ability to live life on mission?

Wrap up the session with any final questions or observations before closing with prayer. Use the next page to record ideas, questions, or prayers.

Complete the personal study in "Three Circles" before the next group session.

PERSONAL STUDY

THREE CIRCLES

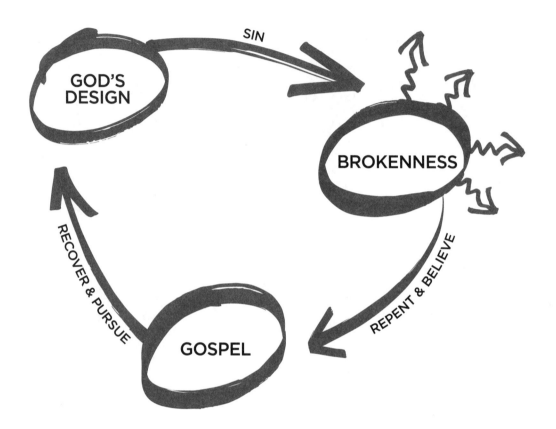

When God restores our relationship with Him, we begin to discover meaning and purpose in a broken world. We can pursue His design in all areas of our lives. Even when we fail, we understand God's pathway to be restored—the same good news of Jesus. God's Spirit empowers us to pursue His design, assures us of His presence in life, and gives us hope of eternal life.

THREE CIRCLES

Everyday missionaries don't just study, learn, and sit around all day reflecting on the gospel in a quiet room. They have an urgency to act by living out their faith in real life. Now we'll transition from solid gospel foundations to strong mission practices.

In studying Scripture—in particular the life of Jesus and the ministry of Paul—we've discerned four clear-cut practices that will help you live on mission:

1. Identify people who need the gospel.

2. Invest in others as you share the gospel.

3. Invite people into disciple-making relationships.

4. Increase disciple making by sending people to make more disciples.

As you study these practices, ask the Holy Spirit for wisdom and insight into how you can pursue them as you join God's mission.

DAY 1
IDENTIFY

You're surrounded by people who need a life-changing relationship with God. You've been entrusted with the gospel, and you know the only way to be reconciled to God is through Christ. Do you see people and circumstances around you with spiritual eyes? Do you see their brokenness?

You're an ambassador for a kingdom that's not of this world. Paul explained what that means for a Christ follower:

> From now on, then, we do not know anyone in a purely human way. Even if we have known Christ in a purely human way, yet now we no longer know Him in this way. Therefore, if anyone is in Christ, he is a new creation; old things have passed away, and look, new things have come. Everything is from God, who reconciled us to Himself through Christ and gave us the ministry of reconciliation: That is, in Christ, God was reconciling the world to Himself, not counting their trespasses against them, and He has committed the message of reconciliation to us. Therefore, we are ambassadors for Christ, certain that God is appealing through us. We plead on Christ's behalf, "Be reconciled to God." He made the One who did not know sin to be sin for us, so that we might become the righteousness of God in Him.
>
> **2 CORINTHIANS 5:16-21**

This week we'll look at four I's that will give you practical ways to introduce Three Circles in your relationships. The first I is identify. Simply identify the people around you who need Christ and then take the time and apply the energy to really know them well.

We all have two broad categories of neighbors: natural and neglected.

Natural neighbors are the ones we typically interact with. They're the most like us in socioeconomic status, level of education, career path, or extracurricular activities and interests. We interact with this group because of our natural rhythms in life—where we live, work, eat, exercise, and so on. To put it another way, we would have to go out of our way to avoid natural neighbors.

Neglected neighbors are people in our community who don't naturally cross our paths. They are "the least of these" Jesus identified in Matthew 25:31-46. We have to go out of our way to interact with these neighbors or at least be intentional about changing our natural rhythm. Right now in your community, your neglected neighbors are struggling, wondering how they'll get through the day.

Identify natural neighbors who need the gospel. Start by naming each of your neighbors, coworkers, etc. You may want to draw a map of your street, using it as a prayer guide and reference.

Anna
marc
marcha + Jamily
my entire Family

Identify neglected neighbors who need the gospel. This will take more effort. First consider people you avoid or find it difficult to be around. Be honest! Next consider areas of need in proximity to your natural routine—hospitals, nursing homes, prisons, youth detention centers, low-income community centers, homeless shelters, or a homeless person you regularly pass while driving.

You're Christ's ambassador, and God is working through you. He has entrusted you with the good news. Pray that God will give you spiritual eyes to identify neighbors who need to be reconciled with Him.

DAY 2
INVEST

Jesus was once asked what the greatest command was. In other words, what's the most important thing for us to do in life?

> "This is the most important," Jesus answered:
> " 'Listen, Israel! The Lord our God, the Lord is One. Love the Lord your God with all your heart, with all your soul, with all your mind, and with all your strength.'
> The second is: 'Love your neighbor as yourself.' There is no other command greater than these."
> **MARK 12:29-31**

According to Jesus, loving God and loving our neighbors are inseparable commands. This is what our lives are all about. This is life on mission.

If we're called to love our neighbors, then without excuse we must know our neighbors. Yesterday you took the first step by identifying exactly who your neighbors are, both natural and neglected neighbors.

The second I is invest: invest your life in the people God leads you to. Paul made clear this part of life on mission when he wrote to the church in Thessalonica:

> We cared so much for you that we were pleased to share with you not only the gospel of God but also our own lives, because you had become dear to us.
> **1 THESSALONIANS 2:8**

Paul declared that, of course, we must speak the gospel to those we identify, but we must also invest our lives—our time, our resources, and our gifts.

How would you describe what it means to love your neighbor as yourself?

Paul also made it clear that investing in others and sharing our lives aren't viewed as work, obligation, or a missions project but a joyful, natural overflow of our relationship with Christ.

When we combine our natural interests or passions with the gospel and use them to build relationships, powerful things can happen. Our passions and the places we live and go can help us identify opportunities to share the gospel.

What are your specific passions and gifts?

What extra resources do you have?

In the left column write the names of the neighbors you identified yesterday. On the right brainstorm ways you can invest in those lives.

IDENTIFY	INVEST

Circle the ideas that seem to be the strongest opportunities and the most enjoyable places to start investing in the lives of your neighbors.

DAY 3
INVITE

The third I is invite. Part of participating in God's mission is inviting broken people to embrace the redemption available through the gospel. Jesus painted a beautiful picture of that idea in His Sermon on the Mount:

> You are the light of the world. A city situated on a hill cannot be hidden. No one lights a lamp and puts it under a basket, but rather on a lampstand, and it gives light for all who are in the house. In the same way, let your light shine before men, so that they may see your good works and give glory to your Father in heaven.
>
> **MATTHEW 5:14-16**

There's never been a city that had a population of one. One person on a hill doesn't qualify as a city, no matter how hard he or she may try. A city is a city because it has a large number of people who make up its population. We're called to invite people into biblical community so that they can experience the "city"—the family of God.

People need to see God's grace lived out among a group of people. They need to see other believers repenting, confessing, rejoicing in God's grace, and forgiving others. They need to see the gospel applied to life. People desperately desire to belong to something bigger than themselves, and despite being more connected than ever through social media, many people are incredibly lonely.

You're aren't meant simply to show off the light of Jesus as an individual. You're also meant to display the light of the gospel through a community of people who are unified in Jesus. Biblical community is like a city on a hill that emits great light to those who are wandering around in a dark, desolate wilderness.

Is your life highly visible to the people you're investing in?

How are they able to see you grow, repent, and change?

Are any of them interested enough in Jesus to come to your group? Consider the names you've already identified and record some ways you would invite them to your small group.

It's a great step to invite people into community. And it's wonderful to have spiritual conversations with them. But always remember that people ultimately need an opportunity to respond to the gospel. This can happen before or after an invitation into community, but make sure you keep your focus on that goal.

Never confuse inviting someone into Christian community with inviting someone into a relationship with Christ. They're both important but not the same. Jesus saves; community doesn't.

How would you invite someone to respond to the gospel? Record sample questions asking people to make a decision about Jesus.

Be ready to use Three Circles this week to invite people into a relationship with Jesus. You may be surprised at what God does when you ask people to respond to the life-changing power of the gospel.

DAY 4
INCREASE

The goal of our mission is not just to have an awesome church, small group, or discipleship group. It's not to keep only the same people around us forever because we like sharing life with them. It's not to selfishly keep what we have.

The goal is to see God move—to see the gospel spread, new people come to know Jesus, and new disciples made. It's to see more people groups reached, more small groups launched, and more churches started in order to invite the broken into biblical community. Jesus instructed His followers:

> The harvest is abundant, but the workers are few. Therefore, pray to the Lord of the harvest to send out workers into His harvest. Now go; I'm sending you out like lambs among wolves.
> **LUKE 10:2-3**

The fourth I is increase. We have an urgent mission: to go out and reap a great harvest of souls, increasing the number of disciples who invest their lives in God's redemptive plan. This mission is literally a matter of eternal life or death.

But we can't accomplish this task alone. Not only does Jesus promise to be with us, sending us in the power of His Spirit (see Acts 1:8), but He also sends the whole church out to increase the harvest.

Jesus commissioned His disciples to "make disciples ... , teaching them to observe everything I have commanded you" (Matt. 28:19-20.) If each new disciple is taught to obey everything Jesus commanded, that includes making more disciples.

We're all called to live life on mission, making disciples wherever we go. And because all disciples are called to make disciples, the kingdom of God grows exponentially. It spreads through multiplication, not addition. Each new disciple grows to maturity and also invites other people to receive the gospel, reproducing more disciples.

Who are the people encouraging you to grow spiritually?

How are they encouraging you to go make disciples?

Who can help you make disciples of the people you've identified on the previous pages?

How can you help other people understand God's invitation to join Him in life on mission?

How could your small group send out people to start new groups in order to reach more people? Would you be willing to lead or host a new group? What's your group's plan for multiplying?

Pray for God to bring a great harvest of new Christ followers. Pray for the courage to be sent, going wherever He leads. Ask God to help you grow in faith and wisdom in order to help others grow in their faith too.

DAY 5
YOUR STORY

Your life has been radically changed by the gospel:

> Once you were not a people,
> but now you are God's people;
> you had not received mercy,
> but now you have received mercy.
> **1 PETER 2:10**

There's no point in dwelling on your old, broken life of sin, but it's this part of your story that makes the gospel such good news. Remembering what life without Christ was like or acknowledging where it was ultimately leading can motivate you to share the good news with others.

Using Three Circles as your guide, describe the way you've personally experienced or come to understand each of the following elements.

God's design:

Sin:

Brokenness:

Repent and believe:

The gospel:

Recover and pursue (your life with Christ now):

"Everyone who calls on the name of the Lord will be saved."
But how can they call on Him they have not believed in? And
how can they believe without hearing about Him? And how
can they hear without a preacher? And how can they preach
unless they are sent? As it is written: "How beautiful are the
feet of those who announce the gospel of good things!"
ROMANS 10:13-15

Boldly proclaim the good news of salvation through word and
deed and watch God work in and through you as you live your life
on mission.

SESSION 5

START

Start the group session with the following question.

Where do you spend most of your time?

After everyone has had a chance to respond, follow up by asking these questions.

How many hours a week do you spend there?

If different from your first answer, where are you most often around people who may need to hear the gospel?

Work.

Transition to the video with the following thought.

With specific places and people in mind, let's start putting all the pieces together for living our lives on mission. In this final session we'll discuss and practice Three Circles as a simple way to engage people in life-changing conversations about Christ.

THREE CIRCLES

WATCH

Follow the notes below as you watch this week's video featuring Jimmy Scroggins.

- Jesus made a way for us to have forgiveness of our sins and a way for God to heal the broken places in our lives.

- The three circles are a conversation guide.

- The three circles give everybody an opportunity to tell our own story.

- The three circles take a conversation about problems or challenges in life and turn it into a conversation about Jesus.

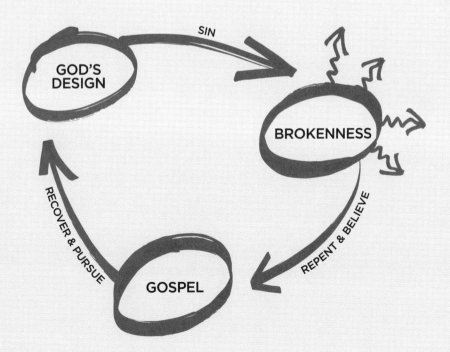

RESPOND

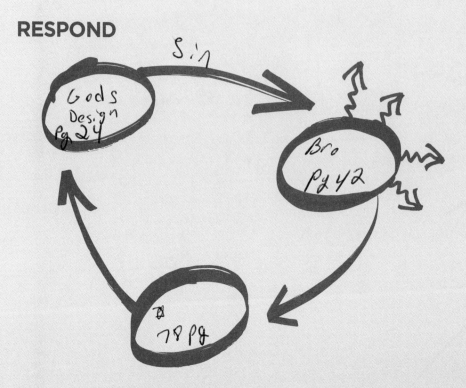

This session is a review of Three Circles. Ask everyone to form pairs and take turns explaining Three Circles to their partner. Practice filling in the diagram and talking about the concepts as you would to a neighbor who had never heard these ideas before. After a few minutes, gather the group together again.

What has been helpful about learning and discussing Three Circles each week?

Has anybody recently had any gospel conversations? If so, how did your personal study or our group sessions help? (See day 5.)

What can be learned from any successes you've experienced in sharing the gospel and living on mission? (See day 5.)

What examples can we learn about what not to do in conversations about the gospel?

Ask three people to read aloud Philippians 2:13; Ephesians 2:10; Colossians 2:6.

Once we've been brought back into a right relationship with God, how do we continually pursue God's design in all areas of our lives?

This week our personal study focused on four I's: identify, invest, invite, increase.

Identify: Who in your life needs the gospel? (See day 1.)

Invest: How will you build those relationships? (See day 2.)

Invite: Have you asked them about their relationship with Jesus? Have you invited them to make a decision about Jesus? Will you ask to meet with them or invite them to your group? (See day 3.)

Increase: How can this group encourage you to live your life on mission? (See day 4.)

Wrap up the session with any final questions or observations before closing with prayer.

Use the next page to record ideas, questions, or prayers.

The following pages provide a review of Three Circles Life Conversation Guide.

GET THE APP, VIDEOS, AND OTHER RESOURCES AT LIFEONMISSIONBOOK.COM

THREE CIRCLES
LIFE
CONVERSATION
GUIDE

We live in a broken world,
surrounded by broken lives,
broken relationships,
and broken systems.

This brokenness is seen in suffering, violence,
poverty, pain, and death around us.

Brokenness leads us to search for a way to make
LIFE work.

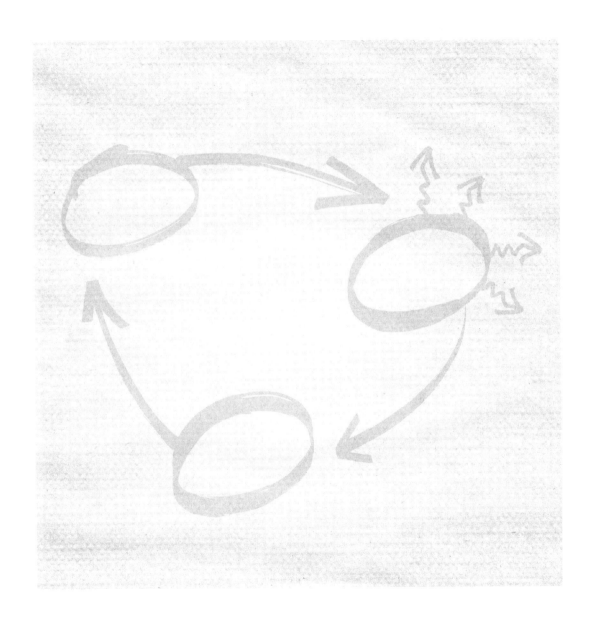

In contrast to this brokenness, we also see beauty, purpose and evidence of design around us.

The Bible tells us that God originally planned a world that worked perfectly — where everything and everyone fit together in harmony.

God made each of us with a purpose — to worship Him and walk with Him.

The Bible says:

"God saw all that He had made, and it was very good" (Genesis 1:31).

"The heavens declare the glory of God, and the sky proclaims the work of His hands" (Psalm 19:1).

GOD'S DESIGN

Life doesn't work when we ignore God and His original design for our lives.

We selfishly insist on doing things our own way. The Bible calls this sin. We all sin and distort the original design.

The consequence of our sin is separation from God — in this life and for all of eternity.

The Bible says:

"All have sinned and fall short of the glory of God" (Romans 3:23).

"For the wages of sin is death" (Romans 6:23a).

Sin leads to a place of brokenness. We see this all around us and in our own lives as well.

When we realize LIFE is not working, we begin to look for a way out. We tend to go in many directions trying different things to figure it out on our own.

Brokenness leads to a place of realizing a need for something greater.

The Bible says:

"They exchanged the truth of God for a lie, and worshiped and served something created instead of the Creator" (Romans 1:25).

"There is a way that seems right to a man, but its end is the way to death" (Proverbs 14:12).

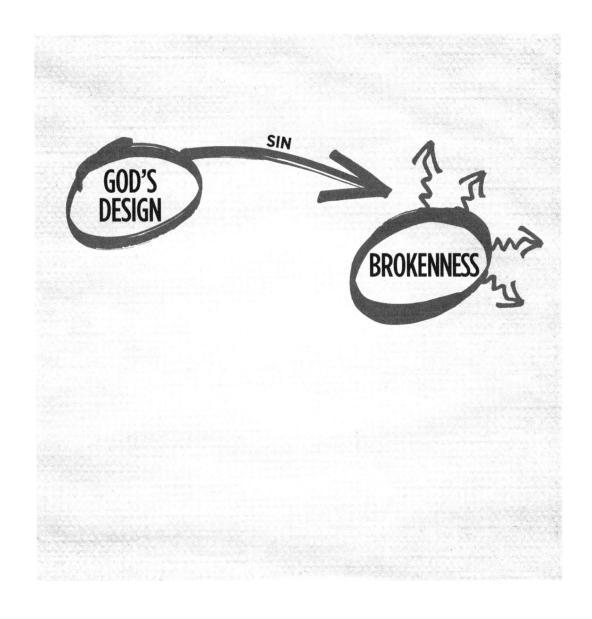

At this point we need a remedy — some good news.

Because of His love, God did not leave us in our brokenness. Jesus, God in human flesh, came to us and lived perfectly according to God's Design.

Jesus came to rescue us — to do for us what we could not do for ourselves. He took our sin and shame to the cross, paying the penalty of our sin by His death. Jesus was then raised from the dead — to provide the only way for us to be rescued and restored to a relationship with God.

The Bible says:

"For God loved the world in this way; He gave His One and Only Son" (John 3:16a).

"He erased the certificate of debt ... and has taken it out of the way by nailing it to the cross" (Colossians 2:14).

"Christ died for our sins according to the Scriptures ... He was buried [and] raised on the third day according to the Scriptures" (1 Corinthians 15:3-4).

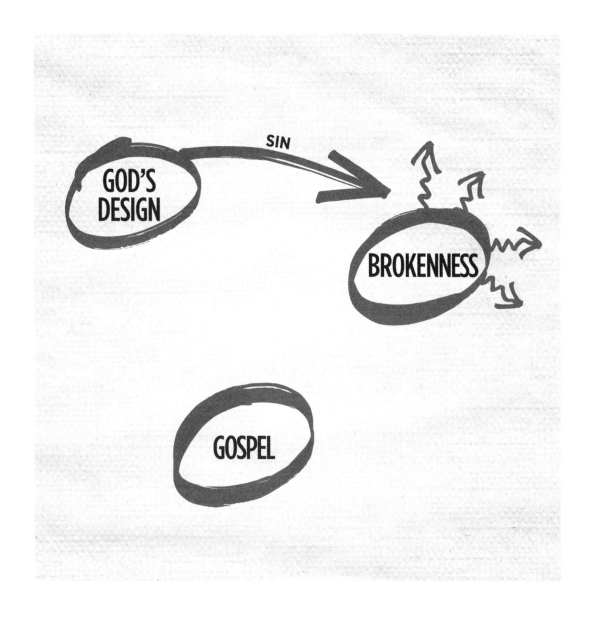

Simply hearing this Good News is not enough.

We must admit our sinful brokenness and stop trusting in ourselves. We don't have the power to escape this brokenness on our own. We need to be rescued.

We must ask God to forgive us — turning from sin to trust only in Jesus. This is what it means to repent and believe.

Believing, we receive new life through Jesus and God turns our lives in a new direction.

The Bible says:

"Repent and believe in the good news" (Mark 1:15b).

"For you are saved by grace through faith, and this is not from yourselves; it is God's gift – not from works, so that no one can boast" (Ephesians 2:8-9).

"If you confess with your mouth, 'Jesus is Lord,' and believe in your heart that God raised Him from the dead, you will be saved" (Romans 10:9).

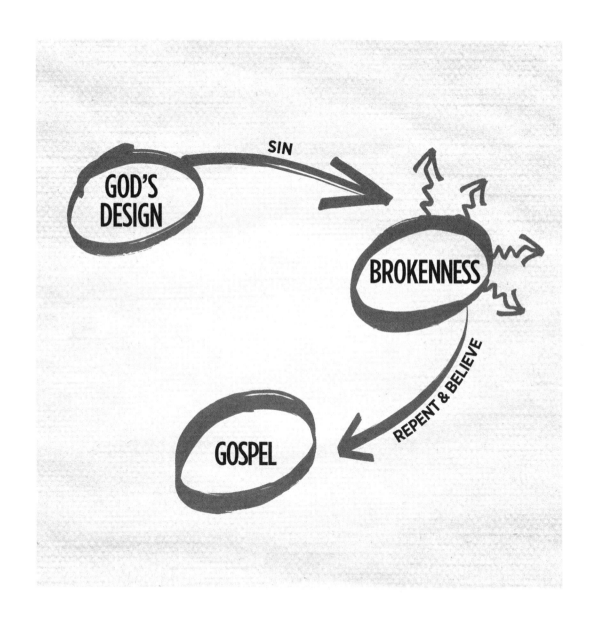

When God restores our relationship to Him, we begin to discover meaning and purpose in a broken world. Now we can pursue God's Design in all areas of our lives.

Even when we fail, we understand God's pathway to be restored – this same Good News of Jesus.

God's Spirit empowers us to recover His Design and assures us of His presence in this life and for all of eternity.

The Bible says:

"For it is God who is working in you, enabling you both to desire and to work out His good purpose" (Philippians 2:13).

"For we are His creation, created in Christ Jesus for good works, which God prepared ahead of time so that we should walk in them" (Ephesians 2:10).

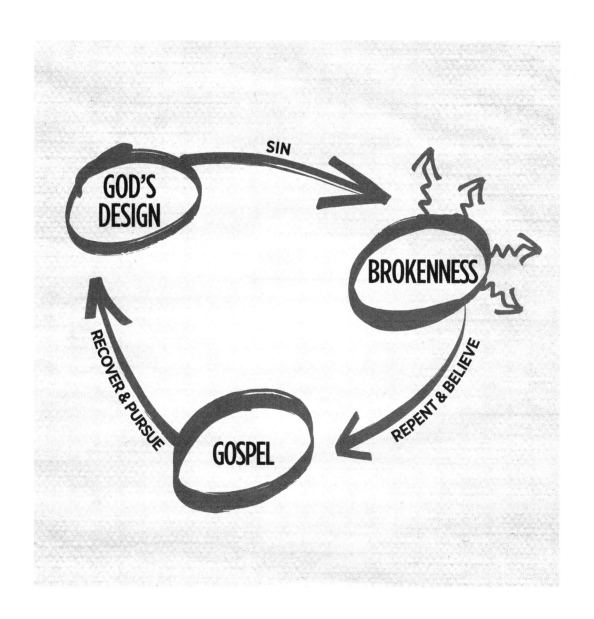

What Should I Do?

Now that you have heard this Good News, God wants you to respond to Him. You can talk to Him using words like these:

My life is broken — I recognize it's because of my sin. I need You.

I believe Christ came to live, die and was raised from the dead — to rescue me from my sin.

Forgive me. I turn from my selfish ways and put my trust in You.

I know that Jesus is Lord of all, and I will follow Him.

The Bible says:

"If you confess with your mouth, 'Jesus is Lord,' and believe in your heart that God raised Him from the dead, you will be saved" (Romans 10:9).

"For everyone who calls on the name of the Lord will be saved" (Romans 10:13).

What's Next?

As we begin our new journey, the Bible teaches us how to pursue God. He has a design for healthy relationships.

Prayer — God wants you to talk to Him about everything that matters to you.

Church — The local church is God's family to help you walk with Him.

Bible — The Bible reveals God's design — showing how to pursue Him.

Share — Now that you have experienced this Good News, tell others.

The Bible says:

"But these are written so that you may believe Jesus is the Messiah, the Son of God, and by believing you may have life in His name" (John 20:31).

"But seek first the kingdom of God and His righteousness, and all these things will be provided for you" (Matthew 6:33).

"Therefore, as you have received Christ Jesus the Lord, walk in Him" (Colossians 2:6).

There is nothing more freeing than
abandoning your own mission and joining

THE *everyday* MISSION *of* GOD.

Life on Mission is a rich but simple guide that will help everyday
missionaries (electricians, lawyers, church planters, students, moms, etc.)
in the areas of gospel and mission, which will lead to an effective ministry
within one's own community. The content is adaptable to any context
and can function well as an individual study or within a small group
environment. *Life on Mission* not only delivers a robust gospel base
with daily mission practices, but is threaded with engaging stories
and powerful questions that help individuals to take
their next steps to living life on mission.

MOODY
Publishers™